IMAGES OF ENGLAND

LOUGHBOROUGH AND SHEPSHED

IMAGES OF ENGLAND

LOUGHBOROUGH AND SHEPSHED

GRAHAM KEMPSTER

TEMPUS

Frontispiece: A worker from John Taylor and Co., bellfounders, of Loughborough, sits inside one of the company's products with a young visitor, in the 1930s. The child doesn't look overjoyed at the experience! John Taylor's founded the massive bell that now hangs in the south-west tower of St Paul's Cathedral.

First published 2004

Tempus Publishing Limited
The Mill, Brimscombe Port,
Stroud, Gloucestershire, GL5 2QG
www.tempus-publishing.com

British Library Cataloguing in Publication Data.
A catalogue record for this book is available from the British Library.

ISBN 0 7524 3252 4

Typesetting and origination by Tempus Publishing Limited.
Printed in Great Britain.

Contents

Acknowledgements

I am very grateful to the following people whose invaluable input and amazing recall of faces and places has helped make this book possible.

In Loughborough: Jo, Barbara, Molly and Colin Swift, Marion Statham, Rhona and Les Henson.

In Shepshed: June Cox, Ben and Joan Burton, Elaine and David Stephenson, Joe and Audrey Bennett, Greta and Frank Mabe, Margaret Pascall.

Special thanks to John Rippin, editor of the *Loughborough Echo*, for allowing access to his newspaper's files.

Graham Kempster
March 2004

Introduction

Loughborough, like every other town, has benefited greatly from the invention of photography in the nineteenth century. For many centuries before this, only sketchy details were recorded of what went on in the town and surrounding area. But, as cameras became increasingly popular, many pictures were taken of local scenes and of people going about their daily life. This fascinating collection of pictures from the past comes from the archives of the *Loughborough and Shepshed Echo*, founded in 1891 and still going strong.

Loughborough, still a market town, is fringed by the Soar Valley on one side and the picturesque Charnwood Forest on the other. Although many new shops have been erected recently, it still retains some of its older buildings. It also still has its twice-weekly market, which draws in shoppers from the surrounding area. It is the second largest centre of population in Leicestershire, after the city of Leicester, and the scale of change that has taken place within the past three decades would have amazed residents from a century ago. It is not only home to many firms, both large and small, but can also boast a university that is known worldwide for its advanced technology and sports science departments.

Many of the pictures in this collection were taken by the late Harold Woods, a long-serving *Echo* photographer of yesteryear who used equipment that was unbelievably ancient by today's standards. He took his pictures with a camera that used photographic plates rather than film and, in his darkroom, he had an horizontal enlarger that was illuminated by a gas light. Yet some of his photos won competitions.

John Rippin
March 2004

Trees being planted by the brook in Forest Road in 1931. As the girls are all wearing the same uniform, they may all be members of the local Girl Guides. Forest Road begins near the heart of Loughborough at the junction of Browns Lane. It then runs south west towards Charnwood Forest and ends at the crossroads with Valley Road and Kirkstone Drive.

one

The Town

Right: Probably photographed about the same time as the picture above, the 'A1 stall' of Green and Co., butchers, of 3 Biggin Street, occupies a prime position around the Fearon Fountain. Some eye-catching advertising is on display, including 'Families waited upon daily', 'We fear no opposition and defy all comers', 'Look at the quality', and an odd one, 'Don't you forget Susan, always buy the ? ?, shop to get it'. The Fearon Fountain was unveiled in 1870 and was paid for by Archdeacon Henry Fearon of All Saints' church, who had campaigned long and hard for Loughborough to be supplied with fresh water. At that time waterborne diseases such as cholera and typhoid were rife.

Above: Market Place on a summer's day in 1901, at 3.45 in the afternoon. A cyclist can be seen near the top of the square, and a carriage awaits its passenger near Waterloo House. The two ladies with the pram seem particularly fascinated by the presence of a photographer, as do the man and young girl to the left. Further down on the left a drayman is seen hefting a barrel from his cart. On the right is James's, once known as the Ship Liquor Vaults and kept by Thomas Bryan. After his death his widow took a Mr James into partnership. He eventually owned the business and the name lived on after his death in 1900. Boots the Chemist built new premises here in 1958. In the distance is what was to become Clemerson's Corner. Clemerson's was a long-established business that sold everything for the home – furniture, bed linen, china, pots and pans etc.

Opposite above: Loughborough Market Place in 1904. The earliest known document relating to Loughborough markets dates from 1221, and there have been markets on this site for many centuries. Fruit and vegetables can be seen on sale in the foreground and, further back, wicker baskets and barrels. Liza Blackwell was a local fruiterer, whose market cry 'Oh they're lovely!' could be heard around the square. She was a well-loved character, and with her plait of dark hair around her head and her shouting she was an awesome sight, certainly quite frightening to some of the children shopping with their mothers. She was, however, an exceedingly generous and benevolent woman and would never see anyone go short or starve, in spite of the size of her own family. Liza lived in Nottingham Road in a two-up-two-down, with the front room used as a fruit and veg shop. In the autumn and winter the market stalls were lit by paraffin flares suspended over the counters, giving a yellow flame just bright enough to illuminate the goods for sale. Prominent in this view is the Lord Nelson public house, affectionately known by the locals as 'the Nellie'. Dorothy Perkins now occupies the building.

The Quorn Hunt meeting in the Market Place on Boxing Day 1920. The first meet was on Easter Day 1894. At the time Lord Lonsdale said that 'they had previously avoided the town because the noise of the spectators alarmed the pack'.

The same soaking wet Boxing Day meet, and a quick stirrup cup for the huntsmen before the off.

The Quorn gathers for a different Boxing Day meet. Although the photograph is not dated, the style of dress suggests sometime in the 1920s. The hunt has not met in the Market Place for over ten years. The Woolworth's building had previously housed Cohen's Bazaar (the Penny Bazaar), followed by 'Woolies' threepenny and sixpenny store. They moved several years later to Keightley's the ironmongers' old site over the way, and more recently to a new store now known as Big W. Next door is Barclays Bank, which still trades from the same site.

The last blacksmith in Loughborough, Percy Brooks, photographed in the early 1930s. He was a jolly man with a large stomach that protruded over his leather apron. He always maintained that he could tame any fiery horse by tying thick twist tobacco into its bit. The smithy was situated in Derby Square and in the garden at the back Percy grew enormous kidney beans, an abundant crop fertilized by hoof parings. After demolition this site became the goods entrance for the precinct shops.

Taken in the early 1930s, this photograph shows the clothing shop of John S. Marr in Churchgate. The tall man in front of the jewellers, in overalls, is a Mr Mottershaw, and to his right, Mr Leon Hall. The sign over the smaller door reads: 'Engagement and Wedding Rings. Present given with every Wedding Ring.'

Bailey and Simpkin, Market Place, March 1926. The large posters at the top of the windows read: 'Buy British Goods. Loughborough Shopping Week. March 15-20 1926. Best of bargains. Plenty of prizes.' In the window on the right with the magnificent glove display is an award announcing it to be the winner of the Window Dressing Silver Cup. The notices with the diamond shapes are the contestants' entry numbers: nos thirty-two (left window) and thirty-three (right window).

Above: The Bull's Head Hotel yard, possibly in the 1880s or 1890s. The men standing are likely to be hotel staff, possibly doorman, ostler, stable lad and porter.

Left: This view of the yard was probably taken some time after the picture above, possibly in the early part of the twentieth century. the only clues are the additional pipework on the left of the building, and the replacement of the old large gas lamp by a more 'modern' one. The flowers in the window boxes and the open windows suggest a warm day, but that doesn't show in the photograph! The buildings seem to be somewhat run-down and scruffy: not a pleasant sight to greet the weary traveller.

THE
BULL'S HEAD
HOTEL.
COMMERCIAL
POSTING HOUSE
T. CARR'S
GARAGE.

Right: The final days of the Bull's Head in June 1927. The boarding projecting out over the pavement must have been to protect passers-by from falling masonry. The first record of the inn on this site was in 1625, although this building dates from around 1724. It was demolished to make way for road widening, after which the licence was transferred to the Bull's Head on the Shelthorpe Estate.

Below: The Road Car Company's first motor bus in Loughborough makes its way along Swan Street in 1910.

Opposite: What appears to be the same bus (D 4782), this time in the High Street by the Bull's Head Hotel and without its 'Arthur Green' advertising board over the cab. Although motor vehicles were becoming a more familiar sight, and the Bull's Head has an AA sign on the wall, the passing bus is still making people stop and stare.

The arrival of this omnibus is causing great interest. Motor buses were still a fairly rare sight on the roads in the days before the First World War. The journeys must have been extremely uncomfortable, with solid tyres and only wooden bench seats to sit on. These omnibuses were later used, during the First World War, as troop carriers to ferry men back and forth from the trenches.

This view of the High Street was taken in 1923, with the Bull's Head sign dominating and more motor traffic in evidence.

Market Place in the 1930s. The road had been considerably widened in the early 1930s, with Burtons, which had a billiard hall on its upper floor, and the other shops forming the new frontage. In the background can be seen Ernest Miller's clothing store, which carried a fine range of ladies' hats. The shop behind the policeman is now a McDonald's. Off to the left is Biggin Street. Luckily for the photographer, traffic in the town centre appears to be quite light, as he seems to have positioned his tripod in the middle of the road. The car approaching is an Austin, with two ladies in the back, driven by a chauffeur in a peaked cap.

This cold, bleak scene was photographed in Swan Street, looking towards Burtons. The shops on the right include Start's the tobacconists, and Smith's confectioners. Today these premises contain a menswear shop, a 'Mini Lab' and a jeans shop. Driving in those conditions at the time must have been quite hair-raising on thin tyres, no heating or demisting, and a single small windscreen wiper (just visible on the middle car). The cyclist looks decidedly unsafe!

Above: Loughborough Shopping Week, 15-21 March 1926. Warner's is certainly joining in with the fun of the occasion, as this mobile billboard shows! Specializing in clothing for the 'slightly older' lady shopper, Warner's was situated on the corner of Churchgate and Fennel Street, a site now occupied by the Left Legged Pineapple CD shop.

Left: Not all vehicles managed to stay in one piece as these 1930s pictures show. Maybe this Morris has tried to take a bend too quickly and toppled over.

The make of car is unknown, but whatever it was it seems to have folded in the middle. Is that a very fed-up owner, in the bow tie, inspecting the damage?

The remains of a bus following some sort of accident. The bodywork of the bus appears to be very fragile and would have offered no protection to the passengers.

STRETTONS
DERBY
ALES
SARACENS
HEAD
INN

WE BUY
OLD GOLD & SILVER
SMITH
COLMANS

Loughborough post office under construction, 1930. The post office on Sparrow Hill was officially opened in February 1930. A concert and ball were held to mark the occasion at the King's Head Hotel, presided over by the head postmaster, Lieutenant-Colonel R.J. Barnes MC R.E. Also attending was the mayor, Cllr A.J. Pilsbury, whose haberdashery shop, Young, Pilsbury and Young, was in the High Street. His premises were demolished in 1927, along with the adjacent Old Bull's Head Hotel, and the business moved into a new shop in the High Street in 1929. It later became Pilsbury and Towle.

Opposite above: Widening of Swan Street in 1931, seen from Derby Square, and looking towards the market. The Saracen's Head and all the buildings beyond were demolished and a new Saracen's Head was built to the left of the old one along with the new *Echo* building. The Offilers pub on the right is the Green Man. Note that a horse-drawn cart is being used to remove the rubble.

Opposite below: Just around the bend from the demolition going on in the previous picture is this image of the actual widening work in its early stages at the corner of Swan Street and Biggin Street. The corner shop was Bennett's shoe shop, now an amusement arcade. Was the handcart used for transporting the builder's tools or taking away rubble?

Right: On 22 May 1932, following twenty-four hours of continuous rain, the Woodbrook was unable to contain the water which swept down from the Charnwood Forest. Several of Loughborough's main streets became flooded. This car is slowly making its way through the town, and hopefully wasn't going fast enough to give the young girl on the right a soaking!

Below: This car, determined to get through, may have been pictured in the Derby Road area. It is thought that the house on the left may once have been the home of the Chapman family, local garage owners. Is the other car parked, or has the engine flooded?

The burnt-out remains of Caldwell's hosiery factory in Churchgate in the mid-1920s. The fire also damaged parts of the infants' department of the nearby Churchgate School. All three departments had to be closed down and the children sent to different schools in the area. Teachers who may still have been at the school at the time include Miss Burnham (d. 1981), Miss Warrender, whose parents kept a faggot shop at the end of Sparrow Hill, Miss Hoare, who was very strict and would pick children up by their arms and swing them into a corner and Miss Margaret, a much-loved headmistress.

Another view of the fire-gutted Caldwell's factory. The premises were never rebuilt and businesses on the site now include an opticians and an office supply company. The cellar is now a car park.

This picture appears to show the demolition of a factory, possibly one of the dye works on the canal, near Fisons, in the late 1920s or early 1930s. The rest of the buildings to the left of the picture seem to be in poor condition, and may have been next in line to be pulled down.

A very bad thatch fire at a row of terraced cottages in Hoton in the 1930s. Amazingly the fireman at the top of the ladder directing the hose is not wearing a safety helmet, only a cap. Two women are watching the jet of water dousing the burning thatch. The one on the left in the white dress is leaning on a tall post and seems to be in a state of some distress, while her friend is there to offer a comforting arm.

Watching a family of swans entering the pond near the Carillon War Memorial in Queens Park in the 1930s. The picture appears to have been taken in warm weather, and it is interesting to note that although the girls are wearing their summer dresses, the adults are still dressed in warm clothes, an overcoat and hat for the lady, suits, waistcoats and flat caps for the men. Queens Park began life as a small Victorian park on 22 July 1889. Sometime between 1905 and 1907 the park was extended to its current size.

This view of the Carillon was most likely taken in the 1960s. The construction of the Carillon was the last significant change to Queens Park. It was opened on 22 July 1923 as a memorial to the dead of the First World War. It is 153ft high and contains forty-seven bells weighing almost 21 tons in total. The grass area at the bottom left is the Granby Bowls Club green. The photograph at the top of this page was taken from the far right of the pond, looking towards the memorial.

An aerial photograph, probably taken in the 1940s, showing the layout of the park and the surrounding areas. The bowling green can clearly be seen at the bottom right, and above it and to the right of the Carillon is the bandstand built to commemorate the Silver Jubilee of Queen Victoria. The cattle market would have been just off the bottom right of the picture. In the lower right corner is part of B.L. Clarke's dye works building, and to the left of the bowling green the black building was formerly covered pig pens. Far left, centre is the Brush FC ground, later to become Loughborough United's ground. The building at centre right with the rounded roof is the memorial swimming baths, now a museum. The area at the bottom left is where the John Storer House now stands. Opened by Princess Margaret on 29 April 1966, the house had three roles: to draw together community organizations, encourage voluntary involvement and to care for the elderly and others in need.

two

Out of Town

No details are available about this lovely cottage, but it is believed to be in Old Woodhouse. The photograph was taken in the 1930s. Compare the condition of this cottage to the run-down one in the previous picture. This seems idyllic: a quiet country road, children playing in the garden and smoke rising from from the chimney pots. Not only has the cottage been recently rethatched, but also on the left, so has the outbuilding (an outside toilet?).

Opposite above: These thatched cottages at Thorpe Acre were sited near to where the Plough Inn now stands. Judging by the children's clothes, the picture appears to have been taken before the First World War.

Opposite below: The same pair of thatched cottages in Thorpe Lane, this time photographed in the 1930s when the Twigg family may still have been in residence. Nothing seems to have been done to improve or modernize them in the intervening years. One of the cottages was occupied from the late 1930s by a Mrs Priestly who was in service at Grange Farm. Her son Albert was tragically killed. The cottages were demolished in the 1950s.

The King William the Fourth Inn, once situated on the A6 at Quorn, and now long since demolished.

Normanton-on-Soar post office in the early 1930s. The building is still there and is now a private residence.

This country lane with a rather unsafe-looking footbridge is in Kings Mills, near Castle Donington. Originally a monastery, a part of the Priest House can still be seen there.

A view of The Green at Mountsorrel. There are no people in the picture to give an indication of the date, but a best guess would be 1920s.

A few notes on the back of this picture from 1883 inform us that it is the commencement of the bridle road at Pignut Spinney in the Valley Road area, leading to the popular beauty spot of Pocket Gate. Why Pignut Spinney? Because at one time pigs were let loose to sniff out the pignuts!

Pocket Gate at the Outwoods. Here at one time was one of the gates used to stop wild animals from the Charnwood Forest getting onto agricultural land. The track appears to veer left beside what is probably a tributary of the Woodbrook and head off to the Outwoods, the outer woods of the forest, and the well-known 'Hanging Stone Rocks'. This was a well-used country path at the time, and the owners of the farm building on the right had put a sign on the wall advertising hot water and teas. A jug of tea could be bought for a few pence, with a penny deposit on the jug of course!

Nanpantan village in 1910 from a postcard to a Mr and Mrs Dolby. It is signed, 'Love Cissy'. The signpost shows 'Golf Links 1, Shepshed 3'. The Longcliffe Hotel stands on the corner of Nanpantan Road and Breakback Lane and was known as 'Jackie Bennetts'. Popular with factory workers, it boasted stabling for eighty horses, a dance room, restaurant and accommodation that could seat 800. It is now the Longcliffe nursing home. Further down, villagers can be seen standing outside houses that once belonged to a Mrs Paget.

The School Cottages, July 1910. The name 'Reggie Gibbins' is written on the back of the picture. The cottages are still there, opposite the school.

Harvesting, probably on Paget's Farm, Nanpantan, 1912. This is another postcard, and again the Gibbins name appears. It has been sent to Miss L. Gibbins, Bedford, and reads 'Dear Louie, I am going to camp on Saturday at half past three. Visiting day is Wednesday. I have been to the choir trip and have spent all the money I had saved. I have left school now. I am your loving Brother, F. Gibbins.' 'L.G.S.' appears in one corner, so young F.G. is likely to have been a grammar school pupil.

three

Events and Celebrations

Children in their character costumes line up for a photograph at a fancy-dress carnival held at St Peter's Sunday School in Storer Road, Loughborough, on 6 February 1934.

A year later in February 1935 another group of children poses for the camera in fancy-dress outfits. Not all the children, in either picture, look pleased at having to stand about in the cold of of a February day.

'Sioux Indians on the warpath!' is the caption on the back of this picture. The 'G' in the window of the Prudential indicates that this was taken at the George V Jubilee Day celebrations in 1935.

Prizewinning babies in classes from under six months up to eighteen months with their proud mums at the Liberal Association's Loughborough Division Grand Fête at Burleigh Hall in September 1929.

A note on the back of this picture reads 'Celebration bonfire on the Beacon'. The style of costume would date the photograph at around the 1880s, so the celebration is perhaps for Queen Victoria's Golden Jubilee in 1887, and taken on Leicestershire's highest point, the 800ft Beacon Hill. This is one of a line of hills on which beacons were lit to forewarn of invading armies.

Opposite above: An outing to a historic monument sometime in the late nineteenth century. There are no clues to help identify the group, but as the majority are ladies it may be a works outing from one of the many hosiery factories in Loughborough. Straw bonnets seem to be the order of the day!

Opposite below: 'Playing Cards'. This photograph, taken on 27 August 1934, shows some girls taking part in what may have been a fund-raising event for the local St John Ambulance. It could have been a 'living whist' game. The girls are thought to be pupils at a local private school, situated behind the Baptist chapel in Charnwood Road, Shepshed, run by a Miss Merriman. The Queen of Hearts is Connie Deacon, one of the two spades visible is Hilda Nelson, and one of the two diamonds is Hilda's cousin, Lily Nelson.

BULL'S HEAD
HOTEL.
COMMERCIAL
AND
POSTING HOUSE
M.A.WIDNALL

GOD BLESS OUR KING & QUEEN

Above: 'Loyal Loughborough': the town turns out to celebrate the Silver Jubilee of George V in 1935. This huge procession is making its way along Market Square, passing Baily and Simpkin, before being directed under the photographer's position (in the billiard hall above Burtons shop) to head back along the other side of the Square. The floats would have been representing the various businesses and organizations of the town.

Opposite above: The flags and banners are decorating the High Street during the celebrations to mark the coronation of Edward VII and Queen Alexandra in 1902. The celebrations ran over three days. On Wednesday 25 June the mayor and mayoress (Cllr and Mrs R. Sutton Clifford) gave a children's fancy-dress ball at the town hall, and in the evening held a mayoral reception. On the following day, the bells of the parish church were rung throughout the day, with a church service at 10 a.m. At 2 p.m. a procession around the town started from Market Square; then the schoolchildren, each wearing a coronation medal, a gift from the mayor, were provided with tea at their schools. In the evening the Grand Coronation Fête and Gala were held in Queens Park, with a huge bonfire lit on Beacon Hill at 10 p.m. On the Friday there was a cricket match between Loughborough Town and Loughborough Park (admission 3d, enclosure 1s) and a dinner at the town hall for the elderly of the town in the afternoon. At 3 p.m. there was another grand procession, including a fancy-dress cycle parade, followed by another fête and gala.

Opposite below: From the same Coronation Day celebration in 1902. The town hall is magnificently decorated, and the men posing for the camera are dressed in their best suits, each wearing a flower in his buttonhole. Further along the street, the building with pillars now houses the HSBC bank.

Another royal day to be celebrated: this time the Coronation of George VI on 12 May 1937. The picture is taken from almost the same position as the previous one, and shows the procession turning at the end of the Square. The decorations strung across the Square are far more elaborate than the 'bunting' that had been used before, but perhaps more significantly it seems that the crowds haven't turned out in the same numbers as for the Jubilee Day in 1935. The only thing that has changed is the installation of a new telephone box.

Opposite below: The mayor, Alderman William Handford, leads the town's dignitaries in a procession past the town hall in 1905, on the way to the grand opening of the Carnegie Free Library. The joint benefactors were Mayor F.R. Griggs and Andrew Carnegie. The entrance, up a few steps in Granby Street, led into a hall, on the wall of which hung a stuffed crocodile. The lending library was straight ahead, and to the left was a reading room with an area in one corner separated by rails labelled 'Ladies Only'. The library was ruled over with a rod of iron by a Mr W.F. Topping. It looked out over Queens Park.

Above: The 1st Loughborough Scouts line up in Fearon Street before the St George's Day parade in April 1935, after which they attended a service at the parish church.

Above: A civic procession passes through the Market Place on its way to All Saints' church for a Jubilee service in May 1935. The policeman on the right in the foreground is PC 41 William Norman, DCM MM. The officer on the other side of the mayor is Sgt Ainsworth. Leading the procession is Mace-bearer Harry Adcock,who served on Loughborough Town Council from 1922 to 1943. Harry served in two wars; he was taken prisoner at Spion Kop (in 1900, during the Boer War) and was wrongly reported as missing, presumed killed in action. It may have been on the day of this photograph that the mayor presented him with a gold watch and a clock. The mayor was Cllr John Shadlock Marr. To his left is the town clerk, Arthur Gwynne-Davies.

Opposite above: The marriage of Tom Insley and Irene Davies at the Baptist church in Baxter Gate, in 1933. Standing either side and behind the bride are her parents, who used to run the Saracen's Head pub (which became the Casablanca). Behind the groom at left is his mother, Eva Insley. Her husband, also Tom, founded Tom Insley's butchers (now Grimleys). His early death meant that Tom junior had to take over the business at the age of sixteen. The bridesmaid on the right is the groom's sister, Marjorie Insley, soon to be married to George Mountrey, who can be seen behind the other two bridesmaids. He was a garage owner in Sutton Bonington.

Opposite below: Trent Bus Co. employees attending the wedding of a colleague at All Saints' church on 14 September 1931. From left to right: -?-, -?-, Harold Bower, Harry Carver, Bill Frost, William Reuben Sands (groom), Harry Hulse, Olive Sands (bride), Bill Haworth, Mrs Haworth, Herb Yates, Ada Sands, Reuben Sands, Syd Tuck, Molly Nield, Eric Atkins, Jack Dilworth, Archie Clarke, Jack Hood, -?-, Harry Postlewaite.

Above: The Loughborough Soar Angling Club team, which won the All England Championship when it was fished on the Soar on 24 September 1932. Some names have been provided, including John (Jack) Hopewell and his brother Tom, Arthur Sutton (a Burder Street chimney sweep), Albert Pervin (upholsterer at Lowe's), Bill Bosomworth (later secretary of the angling club), George Bryant, Tom Uttley (or Utting?), Alf Percival and Charlie Holmes (who ran a maggot factory at Normanton-on-Soar).

Opposite above: A trip on the 'Swan Boat' at Burleigh Brook Park in 1905. Situated off Ashby Road opposite the College Stadium, the park was known locally as either 'Pickleberry Park' or 'Ticklebelly Park', much to the annoyance of the owner who wished to maintain a high moral tone. The entrance fee was 1d. The boat ride cost ½d and was paddled by a man sitting in the 'swan' at the back. With all its passengers aboard it looks very overloaded! Other treats available included a roller-skating rink, a tramcar without wheels, and the swings. 'Burleigh Brook Park, for school treats &c.' was the advertising slogan. 'Apply G. Adcock, 11 Baxter Gate.'

Opposite below: Summer fun in days gone by are recalled in this picture of 'mop fighting' during the Loughborough Boat Club regatta at Normanton-on-Soar in the late 1920s. The burly man brandishing the mop on the left is W.A. Deakin (affectionately known as 'Chubby') of the *Echo*. Under attack in the boat was Horace Harper, a bank employee. Both were old boys of Loughborough Grammar School. Deakin was a champion 'mop-jouster' in the 1920s and was the only contestant to wear socks. When he won so often, comments were made but, as there were no rules anyway, it was deemed okay! The boat club HQ was opposite Chain Bridge with an entrance on Derby Road. Mr Barnsdall the boat builder lived and worked there for many years.

A Christian Fellowship meeting held in Wymeswold, in 1933. The meetings took place every Friday in a loft above a garage attached to the house of a Nottingham doctor. His daughter, Katrina Gilbart-Smith, ran the fellowship, and the girls took it in turns to provide coffee and chocolate biscuits. In the summer there were short trips to the countryside. From left to right, back row: Minnie Spencer, Nancy Goodburn, Amanda Sissons, Clara Collingford, Hilda Brown, Gwen Pitman, Olive Morris (?), Ena Smith, Dorothy Putt, Phyllis Hubbard, Lillian Ovendale. Middle row: Lillian Scarasbrick, Eva Clarke, Doreen Baker, Nancy Bartram, Iris Putt, Katrina Gilbart-Smith, a maid (?), -?-, May Collington. Front row: Millicent Simpson, Florence Collins, Barbara Collingford, Jessie Thompson, Kathleen Savage, Alma Hallam, Mary Brain.

Opposite above: Sileby Adult School Brass Band, winners of a contest held at Humberstone Hall on 12 July 1902. From left to right, back row: E.W. Middleton, A. Freer, C. Wells, J.H. Blower, W.A. Francis (president), J.A. Newbold, G. Owen, J.T. Rose, A. Clarke, C. Lee. Middle row: T.W. Underwood, J.D. Freer, J. Inglesant, J. Freer (conductor), R. Lee, S. Freer, W. Wells, W. Freer. Front row: W. Clarke, W.H. Lee, J.A. Mercy (secretary).

Opposite below: Photographed at the Vicarage garden opposite the church of St Peter and St Paul in Hathern, the winners of a 'Glee Club' singing competition in 1898. All the singers were from the area, and the club was the forerunner of the Hathern Choir. Back row, from left to right: A. Widdowson, F. Swift, T. Morris, ? Burroughs, ? Price, W. Henson, ? Chapman. Middle row: A. Swift, ? Berrington, ? Randon, T. Tollington, ? Price, J. Fisher, A. King. Front: ? Price, W. Hunt.

This wonderful photograph was taken inside the Theatre Royal on its opening night in 1905. The play being staged was *Monsieur Beaucare*. It's not often we see an actor's-eye view of an Edwardian theatre audience. Not a full house, as the uncomfortable-looking bench seats will testify, yet some of the audience will have paid the minimum ticket price and are content to stand at the back of the auditorium.

four

Factory, Rail and Fire

Above: This historic photograph from a reconnaissance camera aboard a Luftwaffe aircraft shows that the Germans thought the Brush Electrical Engineering Co. Ltd factory was a worthy target for bombing. In fact the only bomb to fall on Loughborough during the war was a 250lb one that dropped harmlessly into a field near Parklands Drive, causing little damage except for a few broken windows.

Opposite above: 'Great Paul', weighing over 16 tons, en route from Loughborough to London in May 1882. This huge bell – supposedly the largest in the British Empire – was founded by John Taylor and Co. and hangs in the south-west tower of St Paul's Cathedral. Taylor's is one of the oldest and best-known of Loughborough's industries, and it was here in 1896 that the 'true harmonic' system of tuning bells was rediscovered after the knowledge was lost in medieval times.

Opposite below: This evocative picture, probably taken in the 1880s or 1890s, is inside the workshop of one of the many hosiery manufacturers in the area, Handford and Miller, founded in 1870 by William Handford. At the time of this photograph, production was 2,000-3,000 dozen per week of ladies' hose, and the total number of employees some 300. During the Second World War production turned to socks for the Army and seaboot stockings for the Royal Navy. The site is now Sainsbury's car park.

Loughborough Midland Station in 1888, with two cabs lined up waiting for passengers to emerge. They probably belonged to a Mr Rowe who had stables in Meadow Lane and kept broughams, landaus and cabs, and always met the trains at the station. In front of them is the station's railway coach, the shuttle service of the day. The station today looks very much as it did then, except that the foreground area is now a car park.

A view of the Midland Station from the track side in 1890. The Falcon Engine and Car Works (Brush Electrical Engineering Co. Ltd) dominate the area. The house on the far right was the home of the stationmaster; it later became the general offices. The bridge in the distance gave workers access to the factory and carried a footpath from Glebe Street to the works site and the Big Meadow. It was demolished many years ago. The enamel signs would be much sought after by collectors these days.

Loughborough Derby Road Station in the 1930s, part of the Charnwood Forest Railway, known as the Bluebell Line. The station is no longer there.

Loughborough Great Central Station in the mid-1930s. The Great Central Railway had a line to London that was completely straight all the way. Anything in its path during construction was demolished or moved. Great Central was one of the last railway stations to be built in this country, and one of the first to be closed by Beeching. It is now part of a preserved 8-mile-long steam railway, the only one of its kind to operate on a former main line, and is home to the Great Central Railway Museum, considered by many to be one of the best in the country. Here pipe sections are being loaded onto wagons, destined for the Derwent Valley pipeline. The crane lifting each 3 ¾-ton pipe was designed and built by Morris of Loughborough, whose Empress Works can be seen in the background. Founded in 1897 by Herbert Morris, it was known as the 'Empress Works of Herbert Morris and Bastert'. German-born Frank Bastert gave up his directorship in 1902 and the company became Herbert Morris Ltd.

The wreckage of the 10 a.m. express from Marylebone to Bradford that was passing through Loughborough near the Empress Bridge at about 12.20 p.m. on 31 January 1933. A goods train was being shunted into the sidings and had not cleared the track when the trucks near the back were hit a glancing blow. At least four of the trucks were smashed to pieces, and the express, jumping the rails, eventually became locked with the goods engine.

The fireman of the goods train, Francis George Tarron, aged thirty-six and from Sheffield, was killed. The driver of the express, Thomas Webster, and the ticket inspector, E. Hobson, both of Sheffield, were slightly injured. The only damage to the express was the door to the goods van, and one pane of glass was smashed in the whole train. There were fourteen passengers on the train which consisted of fourteen coaches. The accident occurred only 100m from where the bombs were dropped during the Zeppelin raid of 1916. By a remarkable coincidence 31 January was also the seventeenth anniversary of that awful night.

On 21 Jan 1936 at about 4 a.m., an empty goods train travelling from Rugby to Toton was approaching Barrow-on-Soar when a coupling failed. Half the train was left behind on the line, with the guard, T.F. Busby, the only occupant of the detached wagons, alone in the guard's van at the rear. Shortly afterwards, travelling in the same direction, came the Peterborough to Derby fast train, drawn by two engines. It crashed with terrific force into the rear of the stranded Rugby–Toton train. T.F. Busby, from Cricklewood, was killed instantly, and his body was not recovered for some four hours. So serious were his injuries that he could only be identified by his wedding ring, and a cigarette lighter found in his clothes.

The two engines became derailed and rolled towards the embankment. Both drivers and firemen of these engines escaped uninjured, although the guard of this train sustained cuts and abrasions when he was thrown against the sides of his van. One of the trains was carrying cattle, which escaped from the wrecked trucks, and were later found in a field. Two of the beasts were injured and had to be destroyed.

The Loughborough fire brigade outside the old Free Library in 1888. From left to right, standing: Jabez Cliff (foreman), A. Preston, W. Hammonds, George Clements (superintendent), ? Hopkins, R. Marriott, R. Poole. On the engine: T. Hudson (driver), W. Wesley (foreman), ? Kirk, ? Fletcher, D. Gilbert (turncock), A. Lockwood.

A fire engine from the early 1900s.

An Austin K2 towing vehicle (ATV) from the Leicestershire and Rutland fire service taking part in the Shepshed Wakes parade of 1951.

Photographed at the same event, another representative from Leicestershire and Rutland, this one a Dennis F7 of 1949, the forerunner of today's modern appliance.

No details are available on this photograph, but it looks as though it may have been taken in the early 1900s, and shows a gentleman demonstrating or testing what could be a scale model of a fire engine's extending ladder.

This 1930s Leyland fire engine appears to have been photographed in the 1940s. As the lights have blackout grills on them, and the driver is wearing an army-style helmet we can only guess that it has been made ready for war service.

five

War

Men of the 5th Battalion Leicestershire Regiment line up in the Market Square before heading off to the trenches of the First World War.

More men of the 5th Battalion gather in Queens Park, preparing to follow their colleagues into battle.

On the evening of 31 January 1916 Zeppelins bombed Loughborough. Their long silver shapes with eerie green navigation lights had been seen following the GCR railway line from Leicester, flying up Churchgate, then crossing to the Empress Works, dropping their bombs on the Rushes and Empress Road. To ensure the airships remained stable, bombs had to be dropped from the front and back at the same time. This picture shows the house in which the Page family lived. Mrs Page and her children Freddie and Elsie had just reached their front door when they were killed. Mrs Page's husband was away serving with the RAMC in France. A recently married couple from Thorpe Acre were killed in the Rushes. The wife had just prepared supper and gone out to meet her husband from his work at Empress when they were hit. A woman, standing in her doorway, waiting for her husband to return home to give a friend a banjo lesson, was caught in the blast. Mr Gilbert was killed behind the counter of his shop in Empress Road, and the Bentley family were killed in the doorway of a shop. Ethel Higgs, walking arm in arm along the Rushes with her friend Lizzie, on the way home from Cauldwell's Hosiery factory, had a bomb explode close to them. Ethel was killed and Lizzie suffered a horrific wound just below one knee. She spent several months in hospital, and until her death always had to wear a caliper and spring to walk. One man, out posting a letter, was saved by the thick scarf he was wearing. A piece of shrapnel went through the scarf and lodged in his neck. During air-raid warnings the people attending the Playhouse in Ashby Road (now Sainsbury's car park) were locked in. It was the Playhouse's idea of safety! One of the bombs fell close by. In total that night ten people were killed and eight injured.

Above: Empire Day, Queens Park, 24 May 1930. A celebration of the empire was held every year in Queens Park, with schools from all over the district taking part. Children helped to collect flowers for the 10ft-high cross that is made up from red tulips, may blossom and mauve lilacs. The cross was carried through Queens Park and placed against the War Memorial by children who had lost their fathers in the First World War. A number of them are wearing campaign or bravery medals. On the far left is Dorothy Clarke; second from left is Nora Carpmail, fifth from left Joan Lewis. The boy in front of them is Herbert Sharp. On the other side of the cross, second from left in a pale outfit is Miss T. Baum.

Opposite above: Mayor John Marr hosts a reunion dinner at the town hall in April 1935 for the men of the 1st/5th Battalion Leicestershire Regiment who had served overseas.

Opposite below: A memorial service at the Queens Park bandstand for the fallen of the First World War. The bandstand had been built to commemorate the Silver Jubilee of Queen Victoria in 1887.

This photograph shows the cross being carried by the children through Queens Park to the memorial. Dorothy Clarke is on the right, with a foot almost on the grass, and Nora Carpmail is partially hidden just behind her. Beside Dorothy is Herbert Sharp, and in front of him with a fur collar is Joan Lewis. Miss Baum is on the left at the front, in the white hat.

A different memorial day, but an equally solemn occasion. Behind the cross are children from various schools.

Opposite below: A dull wet day in the mid-1930s as the soldiers of the 5th Battalion Leicestershire Regiment parade through the town on the way to Catterick Camp for their annual training.

Above: After the placing of the cross against the War Memorial a service was conducted, followed by the singing of patriotic songs, like *God Bless the Prince of Wales*, *We Salute Thee and We Pray*, *Bless O God Our Land We Pray*, and songs appropriate to England, Ireland, Scotland and Wales, such as *Jerusalem*, the *Londonderry Air*, *Bluebells of Scotland* and *Land of My Fathers*. The Union Flag was saluted, and afterwards a loud cheer went up as the mayor announced the children could have the rest of the day off as a holiday.

'A' Company Home Guard, summer 1941.

Opposite above: How to deal with a firebomb: a demonstration at Brown's Lane Brush football ground in autumn 1939. The war required much effort from volunteers, and newly formed bodies included the Women's Voluntary Service, the Local Defence Volunteers (renamed the Home Guard), Air-Raid Precautions and the Auxiliary Fire Service.

Opposite below: More volunteers, this time to help with sandbagging the windows of the old Loughborough General Hospital in Baxter Gate on 3 September 1939. Youngsters from the town were always willing helpers when it came to filling the sandbags.

Officers of the 9th (Loughborough) Battalion, Leicestershire Home Guard, photographed outside Hazlerigg Hall. The commanding officer, Lt-Col. S.K. Lewis, is seated at the centre in the front.

six

Sport

Above: A game of billiards at a newly opened club in Loughborough, April 1935. Third from the left is Bill Mitchell, secretary of the Loughborough and District Billiards League. He was an employee of Herbert Morris Ltd. Second from the right is believed to be Walter Hassall, a fitter and engineer at H. Morris, and fourth from the right is Tom Hassall.

Left: Jack 'Boris' Brown, the Loughborough Boat Club entry for the Diamond Sculls at a Henley Regatta, mid-1930s. In his left hand he holds the Challenge Cup, but whether this is a Loughborough cup or a Henley cup is unclear. Jack was the son of Owen Brown, whose company still provides marquees for hire.

This dramatic action shot shows Beggars Maid about to unseat his jockey in the 1934 Midland Hunters Steeplechase at Loughborough Racecourse on Derby Road. The winner of the race was Miss Mary, in the centre. The buildings in the background are Tommy Shepherd's farm.

The opening of the new Farnham Tea Room at the Quorn Cricket Club ground in August 1934. Mrs Farnham of Quorn Hall, who performed the opening ceremony, is seen here receiving a gold key from the architect. Bungalows have now been built on this site.

Trophy winners at the Loughborough College swimming gala, June 1934.

Above: Motorcycle racers push-start their machines uphill at a wintry race meeting at Donington Park in the 1930s.

Below: A line-out in a match between Loughborough College and Coalville Rugby Club in February 1934.

J.F. Michie straddles the bar at 5ft 10in to win the high jump at an athletics meeting in September 1934.

H. Eldon Hope of Leicestershire clears the bar easily in the pole vault at the same athletics meeting in September 1934. The landing area doesn't look very soft!

Young athletes pose for the camera after the 1935 Junior College sports. Holding the large cup is H.P. Adcock. It was the 'Block Cup' and was presented by the father of an older boarder to the best athlete of the year. The photograph was taken in front of the sports pavilion on Ashby Road playing fields, next to what is now Epinal Way. The pavilion was built in 1921, and demolished in 1965 by the Ministry of Transport, which had to pay £38,000 in compensation. It is believed to have been built by the students as part of a 'training on production' scheme. They were paid a cup of tea and a bun in the morning, and the same in the afternoon. From left to right, back row: Holmes, Gray, Winters, Meeklam, Wain, Hammond, Goodacre. Middle row: Lewin, Baguley, Houston, Scott, Richards. Front row: Gilkes, Eaton, Purdy, Adcock, Godwin, Bladon, Weatherley, Staples. Bladon's father was in charge of the garage at the old technical college. His boss was Dr Schofield, one of the men responsible for founding the current university. Godwin's father is thought to have run a bookmakers in Leicester.

A unique photograph of three civic heads of Loughborough enjoying a game of bowls in June 1937. Second from the left is Cllr Frederick George Fleeman (deputy mayor), to his left Cllr Arthur Lacey (mayor), and on the far right Cllr John Shadlock Marr (former mayor).

The Station Hotel Bowling Club team, 1934/35. The club won the Hartopp Cup with a score of 69 shots up. It was a successful year for the team, as they came third twice and gained a fourth place in another bowling competition; they had a record season, losing only three matches. From left to right, back row: J. Foster, J. Long, H. Ironman, A. Yeomans, W. Smith, Sam Wilson, Stan Wilson, T. Cartwright, C. Wall, L. Musso. Front row: J. Kerfoot, A. Ponder (honorary secretary), J.B. Hammersly (captain), E. Lacey (president), R. Tipping, T.W. Sykes.

The Granby Bowling Club beats the Station Hotel Bowling Club at their own green, 27 April 1934. Matt Measures, a popular 'skip' with the Granby team, is directing his end. In the previous season Granby had won two trophies and Station Hotel one.

Members of the Granby Bowling Club pose with their trophies, 15 September 1934. From left to right, standing: S. Clarke, J.H. James, William Daws (landlord of the Saracens pub), W. Adcock, S. Millington, W. Turner, E. Concannon, A. Hammonds, F. Wignall, J. Carpmail, F.W. Stephens, H. Hoare, W. Strutt. Sitting: A. Dalby, F. Knifton, P. Bird, H. Chester (honorary secretary), H. James (captain), M. Measures, E. Garram, W. Cunnington. Kneeling: H. Sheffield, J. Adams, -?-, -?-, -?-.

J.A. Hartopp presents the Hartopp Cup to Matt Measures of the Granby Bowling Club, Green Park Road, 16 September 1933. The very tall man to the right of the picture in the striped suit is the runner-up, E. Concannon, also of Granby.

Opposite above: Loughborough Corinthians FC, winners of the Leicestershire Junior Cup, 1900/01. From left to right, back row: Mr A.E. Moss, Mr W. Crow, Dr Phelps (chairman), Mr J. Paget, W. Noon, T.H. Bumpus. Middle row, standing: A.J. Shepherd, N. Mercier, J. Ratcliffe, C. Moss, A.E. Shaw, G.E. Bailey, T. Trees. Sitting: E. Harding, C. Gadsby, G.F. Brewill, T. Ainger, A. Moore. Front row: L. Kidger, A.F. Palmer, B.C. Appleby.

Opposite below: Loughborough Corinthians Amateur Football Club, second team, 1901/02. From left to right, back row: Tom Trees, C. Gadsby, W. Crow. Middle row, A. Harding, H. Paget, H. Merriman, E. Marston, H. Green, Dr Phelps. Sitting: W. Matthews, E. Palmer, G.F. Brewill, T. Tilson, O. Roberts, E. Stevens. Front: A.J. Shepherd. The Corinthians were formed in 1896 and first played on the Glebe Street ground, having to use rooms at the Lonsdale Hotel to change and wash, then moving to the Browns Lane ground. Their first fixture was on 5 September 1896 against Loughborough Park. They lost 4-0. The team's final match was on 21 April 1934, when they sensationally beat Leicester City Reserves 2-1 in the final of the Leicestershire FA Senior Cup. The team on that occasion was Jones, Chambers, Stout, Davison, Shepard, D'vry, Greenfield, Durnelow, Sharp, Orton, Weston.

Loughborough Wednesday Football Club, 1900/01. At one time all the shops in town closed on Wednesday afternoons, so the men who wanted to play football, but couldn't on a Saturday because of work, formed a 'Wednesday' team, with games played on those afternoons. From left to right, back row: H.W. Baggaley (captain), J.C. Stinson, H.A. Pilsbury. Middle row: H. Rose (trainer), E. Wyatt, H. Dorman, S. Carte (vice-captain), H. Ball, E. Beeby (referee). Front row: T.C. Carpmail, H. Cashmore, J. Adcock, C.W. Tyler, H.P. Simmons.

seven

Big Houses

Above: The 1730 Triumphal Arch at Garendon Hall, a folly that remains to this day. This photograph dates from the turn of the twentieth century: are the men posing for the camera workers on the estate, or maybe a group on a day trip from the town?

Opposite above: Garendon Hall, erected by Samuel Phillips in the middle of the eighteenth century, stood on the site of a Cistercian abbey founded in 1133, and was the home of the De Lisle family. The hall was used by the Army during the Second World War and was badly neglected. It stood empty for many years before its demolition in 1964. The rubble was used as hardcore for the M1, which was being built through Leicestershire at the time.

Opposite below: The homecoming of the De Lisle family on 26 June 1907. Due to the financial difficulties of Everard De Lisle's grandfather, the family had been forced to let the hall to the Marquis De Salico and then to a Mr Lucas Tooth.

Old Knightthorpe Hall was demolished in 1968 to make way for Knightthorpe Court flats and a new public house, the Gallant Knight, afterwards renamed the Maltings. The hall was once far bigger than shown in this photograph; at the time of the photograph a Miss Mosely, at one time a teacher at Limehurst School, lived on the upper floor of the house. A former newspaper delivery boy could remember Miss Mosely lowering a bucket on a rope to put the papers in.

Whatton House at Long Whatton near Kegworth, home of the Crawshaw family. During the Second World War pregnant mothers from the big cities such as Nottingham and Birmingham were evacuated here for safety. In one tragic incident a maid from the house was killed when a stricken Luftwaffe bomber jettisoned its bombs in Mill Lane before crashing into nearby fields. The German crew of four were also killed, and are buried at Burton-on-Wolds.

eight

Mayoral Duties

Mayor John Marr joins his guests, all unemployed men, at the town hall on the evening of 16 March 1935.

Cllr Marr surrounded by his team of willing helpers at the same supper for the unemployed. Standing third from left is Albert Brooks; his mother, Rose Brooks, is at the far right of the middle row; and their next-door neighbours, Mr Pat Weston and Mrs Weston, are standing seventh from right and third from right.

The mayor and mayoress, Cllr and Mrs John Marr, join the dancers for a photograph at a Jubilee ball to celebrate the twenty-fifth anniversary of George V's coronation, on 12 May 1935. John Shadlock Marr was mayor twice, first in 1933/34 and again in 1934/35. As well as his clothing and jewellery shops in Churchgate, John Marr also ran a pawnbroking business (he was called 'Everybody's Uncle'). His customers could be seen on a Monday morning bringing in suits to pawn, and redeeming them again on Friday for the weekend. His wife had a hairdressers at the bottom of the Market Place.

Mayor and Mayoress John and Mrs Marr judge a May or Carnival Queen and attendants in Queens Park in the mid-1930s.

A group in the Mayor's Parlour at the town hall on 28 November 1937, on the occasion of the Leicestershire Yeomanry dance. Included in the picture are the mayor and mayoress, Alderman and Mrs Arthur Lacey, Cllr Marr (standing third from the left), his daughter Doris to his left, and Mrs Marr standing behind the mayor. Also in the picture are Col. Martin, Col. Tilney and Maj. Tilney.

Mayor Arthur Lacey attends a Loughborough Students Representation Council Dinner in 1937. With him are, on the back row, Mr Young (president) (far left) and the college principal, Mr W. Birrel (far right).

Cllr Arthur Ernest Armstrong, mayor of Loughborough, laying the first stone of the Loughborough Methodist church extension in 1921.

Cllr William Pownall Stagg hands over the key at the opening of the Shelthorpe Social Club in 1949 to Arthur Cope, its president. Alderman Stagg pulled the first pint. Also in the picture are Mrs Connie Usher, wife of the town clerk Arthur Usher, Edward (Ted) Millage (secretary of the social club), Wilf Farrett Dew (treasurer) and Percy Harold (trustee).

The Loughborough Lady Clerks' Leap Year Ball in 1928, apparently attended by two mayors and mayoresses. The mayor and mayoress of Loughborough, Cllr and Mrs Alan Moss, are on the left of the dignitaries, but there is no indication as to who the others may be. At the back the band is ready for the 'Paul Jones', a dance in the course of which each man takes a number of partners in succession.

nine

Schools

The school cricket team, 1930/31. At the left of the back row is Sepp Atterbury, coach and groundsman, who worked at the school during the summer term, but during the winter was trainer for Plymouth Argyle FC. From left to right after him, back row: P.H. Allen, ? Sooby, Tom Wagg, -?-, Mr Mander, -?-, G.H. Saunders, ? Dexter, -?-, S.R. Pullinger (headmaster). Sitting: J. Saxton, Walter Mason, ? Coe, Arthur Mant, -?-, Jim Manning (who went on to become sports editor of the *Daily Mail*), -?-. On the ground: Peter Twells.

Opposite above: A lovely summer's day in the 1930s, and pupils and their parents enjoy afternoon tea in the sun at Loughborough Grammar School.

Opposite below: The new gymnasium at LGS in February 1935. The old gym had been converted into classrooms, and as a result PE had been taking place outside. Because of the increasing importance of PE the governors had decided that a new building was essential. A wooden building with russet-green tiles, to blend in with nearby trees, was built on the west side of Burton Walks.

Tennis practice for the girls of Loughborough High School in the mid-1930s.

Above: The girls of the high school photographed at what is thought to be a speech and prize-giving day in the late 1930s. Among the girls featured in this picture are: Mary Marshall, Edna Cheals, Margaret King, Dorothy Kemp, Lesley Hale, Gwenda Swain, Joyce Edwards, Beverly ?, Grace Coupe, Barbara North, Enid Hooper, Mary Cumberland, Margaret Ward, Eileen Caldwell, Toni Godfrey, Sheila Spencer, Dinah Holt, Maevi Cursley.

Opposite below: Churchgate School football team in 1930/31, the year that they won the Loughborough Schools Senior Cup. This must have been the school's last football team before its closure in 1930.

Above: Teaching staff at Limehurst Secondary School, 8 May 1931. This was the school's official opening, following the closure of Churchgate School in 1930. From left to right, back row: Tommy Webster (science), Miss Gardener (history and needlework), R. Ledbury (woodwork), Miss Jenkins, R. Hallam, Miss Barbara Upton, Mr Walker, Tommy Pritchard (music), Joe Maxwell. Middle row: Miss Agnes Chester (deputy head, arts and crafts), Miss Cartwright, Miss Nunn, Miss Cox, Miss Vera Savage. Front row: Mr Kirk, Miss Clayton (domestic science), Mrs E.M. Handford (girls' headmistress), Cllr Dawson (chairman of the Education Committee), Mr J.H.W. Matthews (boys' headmaster), Miss Peggy Austin (history), Mr Eggleston. Originally, the girls were taught at one end of the building and the boys the other; later the school became a single-sex establishment, but it has since reverted to co-educational teaching. Pupils come from the junior school to Limehurst before moving on to Burleigh Community College.

Rendell Street School football team, 1934/35, photographed on 15 April 1935. From left to right, back row: Mr Green (headmaster), Mr Hammersley. Middle row: Baguley, Mercer, Hardy, Ward, Giles, Burns. Front row: Dakin, Hallam, Selby, Eggleston (captain), Collington, Oliver.

Students study quietly in the library at Humphrey Perkins School, Barrow-on-Soar, in the 1950s. The Revd Humphrey Perkins is rightly considered the founder of the school, although the Revd Benjamin Bewick may be considered a co-founder, and the man responsible for bringing the school into existence was the Revd Vere Foster, vicar of Barrow. The school was ready to receive its first pupils in 1735 under the headmastership of Mr John Oliver of St John's College, Cambridge.

ten

Shepshed Wakes: July 1950

Specialists in
POULTRY HOUSES
FARM BUILDINGS

Phone :
SHEPSHED
2393

R. V. WEST LIMITED

Timber Merchants and
Sectional Building Manufacturers

Regd. Office:

ASHBY ROAD, SHEPSHED

WE INVITE YOUR ENQUIRIES FOR ALL YOUR NEEDS IN SECTIONAL BUILDINGS

Store Sheds, Poultry Houses, Pig Huts
Garages, Summer Houses, etc., etc.

Send for our Catalogues

Above: Organizer and chairman of the Wakes, R.V. (Ron) West, at the microphone. The event was sponsored by the local War Memorial Committee and raised £500 to renovate and modernize the War Memorial and move it from the Market Place to a site at Glenmore Park. The thatched building in the background was the Bull's Head, and the landlord at the time was Wilf Whitmore. Occupying the premises now is a hairdressing salon. Ron West was a local businessman (sectional building manufacture) and chairman of the British Legion.

Left: Ron West's advertisement in the 'Wakes' souvenir programme.

Opposite below: Lee Savold chats with (right) Ron West and (second from right) possibly J.D. Robertson, the parade secretary. The third man from right, in glasses, is Howard Bell.

Above: R.V. West invites the world heavyweight boxing champion, Lee Savold, who beat Bruce Woodcock, to open the proceedings. Savold was accompanied by his manager Bill Daly and sparring partner Pat McComisky. Lee expressed the wish that 'never again would it be necessary for British and American soldiers to have their names on a memorial such as this'. He was then presented with an inscribed scroll and a gold fountain pen. In the background at the far right is a St John Ambulance man, Albert Millar, himself an amateur boxer.

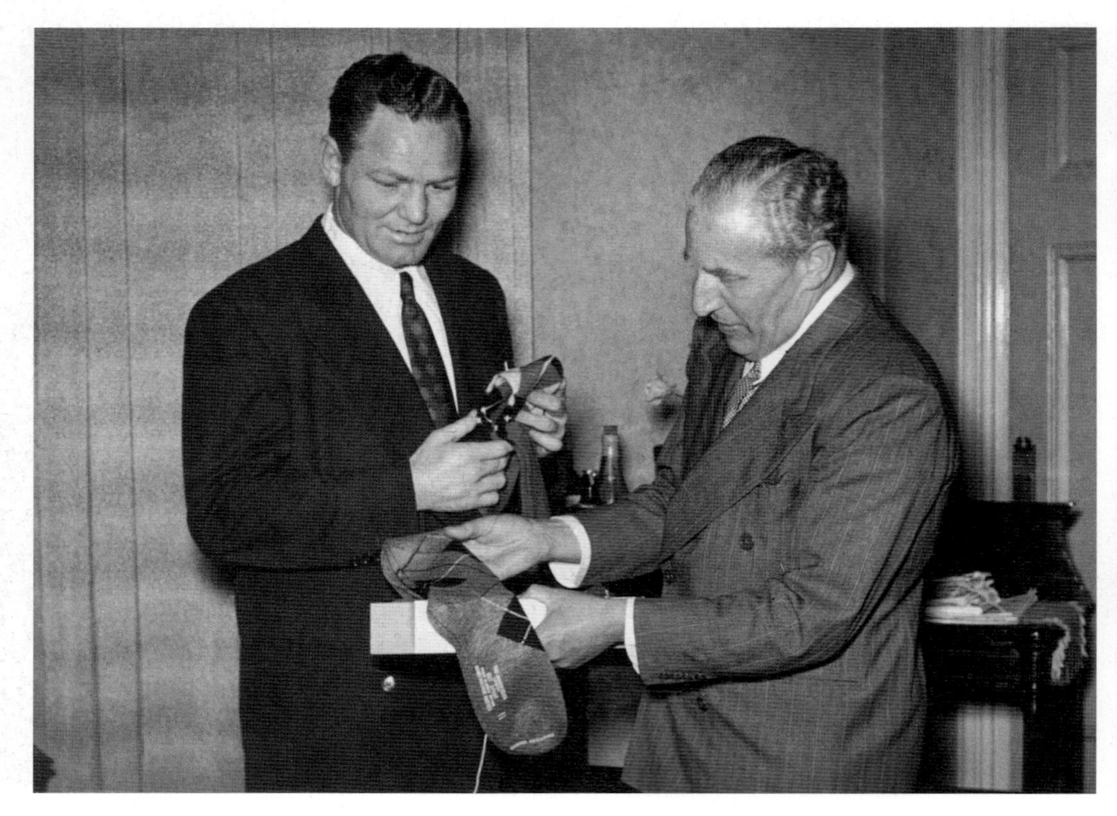

Previously, at a luncheon at Hathern in his honour, Lee Savold was presented with Argyle socks by Eric Gibbs, director of the manufacturing company. Shoes for the boxer's wife were also presented on this occasion, possibly from George Green and Sons.

Before the parade some of the crowd are entertained by a fancy dress 'character'. The man standing to the left of the picture with an open-necked shirt is Stan Sherwood, with his wife Dorothy on the left, in the dark jacket. Their children, Pat and Graham, are standing immediately in front of them. Stan worked in the packing department at Gibbs. The tall man behind the 'character' is Derek Chantrill. Of the boys sitting at front left, third from left (tall) is Terry Bradbury, and fourth is Tony Beck. On the right of the picture the three older boys standing are, in open-necked shirt, Roy Quemby; next to him in dark suit, Donald Allen; and, wearing the fancy tie, John Wright. Just visible in the background, parked outside the Blue Ball (with the Offilers Ales sign) can be seen the Barton's bus which ran an hourly service between Nottingham and Coalville.

Above: The crowd is eager to see the world boxing champion. The lady just visible in the picture at bottom left is Florence Lester, while the lady in glasses, pointing, is a Mrs Hibbert. The little girl next to her, waving, is Glenys Hewitt. The St John Ambulance man is Walter Cramp. The lady at the lower far right in glasses is possibly Lois Wardle. The gates in the background were the back entrance of the post office.

Left: Jackie Morgan of Thringstone had the honour of leading the parade. He was a regular at all the local fêtes and carnivals, and always with a different costume. The pub top right is the Blue Ball.

A general view of the Market Place. So many people had turned out that the police had great difficulty in clearing the way for Lee Savold's car, and as a consequence he was half an hour late.

The parade gets under way. Headed by the Town Silver Prize Band, the tableaux from the factories and organisations progress from Market Place to Loughborough Road, Forest Street, Leicester Road, Cambridge Street, Oxford Street, Charnwood Road, Springfield Road, The Meadows, Lambert Avenue, Garendon Road, Kirkhill, Bull Ring, Field Street and back to Market Place for the judging. In this horse-drawn trap are, from left to right, ? Webster, Phyllis Baxter and Flo Bird.

This is 'Nursery Rhymes', by the office staff of Joseph Harriman Ltd, passing along Brook Street. The sections are, from left to right, 'Little Boy Blue', 'Queen and Knave of Hearts', 'Little Bo Peep'. The people are, from left to right, Audrey Hoyle, Iris Spacey, Brenda Cartlidge, -?-, -?-, -?-, Margaret Wallam, June Bell and Dorothy Wignall.

In the top window, looking down at 'Arabian Nights', from Clarke's Boxes, is Mrs Mawby, from the butchers J.B. Mawby. The butchers were well known for their faggots. All you had to do on a Monday was to take your dish or can along and have it filled with fresh, home-made faggots and gravy. Tuesday was for chittlings and tripe was served on Friday. Florrie Morby (their daughter) became organist at Shepshed Methodist church. The shop is now used by an office cleaning company.

Here are the girls from Harriman's second float, entitled 'Gypsy Encampment'. From left to right: Phyllis Spence, Margaret Lakin, -?-, Christine Walker, Margaret Hill, May Martin, Joan Hartshorn, Joan Hillier, Eileen Morris.

'Summertime' from Gibbs of Shepshed Ltd. The ladies are, from left to right: Margaret Brooks, Enid Hopewell, Greta Cartlidge, June Betts. One of the little girls is thought to be Margaret Davie, whose family ran the Lifeguardsman (now known as the Gobbin) on Hathern Road. Second from left, with hands together, is Kathleen Morley. All the woodwork for the Gibbs floats was made by Bert Gent, a carpenter with the company. The lorry was from William B. Haywood of Shepshed.

A second picture of 'Summertime'; in this one Greta Cartlidge can be seen better second from the right.

This one is 'Cherry Ripe' from George Green and Sons, shoemakers. Far right in the bonnet is Freda Briers, and third from the right is Freda Hodgkinson. Third from left is Audrey Pollard. The lorry has been supplied by F.S. (Freddy) Mee, a well-known local farmer, who was said to have grown some of the biggest 'cow cabbages' ever seen. Only one or maybe two would fit on the back of his lorry! After the Wakes judging, the carnival would move off to one of Freddy's fields for the evening merriments. The site where George Green's factory stood is now the Willows nursing home.

An 'Old English Garden', with the girls from George Braund Ltd. From left to right, looking over the back of the lorry is Dorothy Bell, then Kath Mackenzie, Stella Bradbury and Mavis Jarvis.

A pause for a photograph outside A.V. Matlock Ltd for 'Rose Garden', representing Lacey's of Shepshed Ltd. Leaning against the lorry is the driver, Gus Allen. The little girl at far left is Pearl Wheeldon. Matlock's building now houses Simpson's (farm supplies etc.).

Another garden tableau, this one the 'Old English Garden' dray from C.W. Halls Ltd, at one time the biggest manufacturer of socks in the country. First on the left is Pat Stocks. Their happy banjo player is Clifford Newton. Cliff can still be seen on his cycle around the town.

Stopped outside the Crown Hotel, but with no time for a refreshing dram, are 'The Bonnie Bells of Scotland', from John Scott-Nicholls. The man standing near the back of the dray is Harrold Berridge, chief marshal for the parade. He was a well-known Trades Union official for the hosiery industry and worked at Braunds. Standing to the left of the cab in a light suit is Bernard Elliot. Sitting at the centre of the tableau is Margery Fardell, and sitting on the right is Margery Jordan. The lorry was supplied by Johnson Metals. Housing now stands on their former site.

'The Rainbow', and under it are the girls from Wolsey Ltd. Another of Freddy Mees' lorries is in use here. It has been possible to identify a few of those pictured. Second from the right, in stripes and with a big smile is May Smith, who was evacuated from Sheffield during the war, and stayed on! Third from the right, with dark hair, is Jean Danvers, and next to her is Doreen Scaysbrook. Between Jean and Doreen, standing at the back, is Audrey Scaysbrook. Just behind May is Marion Stocks. Elsie Wale is second from the left and next to her, looking over her shoulder, is Connie Spence.

Ready for the judging to begin are the 'Purity' girls from Wightman and Tapp. Marie Elliot is at front centre; at front right, Margaret Corbett; behind her, Dorothy Webster; and at far back Valerie Hutchinson. At front left is Peggy Baxter and behind her is Jean Evans. Behind Marie at the back is Joyce Luddon.

Opposite: Another Gibbs' dray. This time it is 'Swiss Weather House', with more fine carpentry work from Bert Gent. The girls were chosen for their particular hair colours. On the left, in the 'wet' door is Jean Carter, whose hair was jet black, and in the 'fine' door is Margaret Walker, whose hair was white blonde. The girls were on a revolving platform, so as one came out, the other went in!

WET
Chez-Nous
FINE

Lacey's of Shepshed 'Rose Garden' again. Brenda Birkenshaw is in black at rear centre, bottom left seated is Pearl Wheeldon and at bottom right is ? Wilcox.

Opposite above: 'The British Empire' from Tomlinson and Riley, shoe manufacturers. We can see representatives from all over the empire, watched over, of course, by John Bull. The face colouring may have been 'Burdells Gravy Salt' which could be bought in block form in its distinctive yellow packaging (rather like a large Oxo cube), and was used for flavourings, gravies etc. It has not long vanished from our shelves.

Opposite below: This fantastic tableau is 'The Bonnet', a horse-drawn entry from Arthur Deacon and Co. Ltd. This huge bonnet seems to have been made entirely of woven basketwork, and must have taken many days to complete. If this wasn't the winner on the day, what on earth could have beaten it? At the back in the centre is Dorothy Allen; in front of her to the left is Jean Underwood and to the right, Jean West. Middle row: Cath Crowson, Susan Lakin, Cath Unwin. At the front only Pauline Deacon, on the left, can be identified. The St John Ambulance man is George Stanley from Long Whatton.

L

SPORTS AND COMPETITIONS

Stewards: P. MILLER, Esq. and C. MEE, Esq.

CHILDREN:

Event 1.—Egg and Spoon Race (aged 5—7 years).
Event 2.—Obstacle Race (aged 8—10 years).
Event 3.—Wheelbarrow Race (aged 11—14 years).
Event 4.—Obstacle Race (aged 5—7 years).
Event 5.—Three-Legged Race (aged 8—10 years).
Event 6.—Obstacle Race (aged 11—14 years).

ADULTS:

Event 1.—Ladies. Egg and Spoon Race.
Event 2.—Gents. Sack Race.
Event 3.—Ladies. 100 Yards (for those over 60 years of age only).
Event 4.—Ladies and Gents. Three-Legged Race.
Event 5.—Gents. 100 Yards (for those over 60 years of age only).
Event 6.—Ladies and Gents. Wheelbarrow Race.

ANKLE COMPETITION FOR LADIES OF ANY AGE.

Details will be given over the loudspeaker.

MEN'S BEER DRINKING CONTEST.

Details will be given over the loudspeaker.

MEN'S KNOBBLY KNEE CONTEST.

Details will be given over the loudspeaker.

BALLON RACE.

For one week prior to the parade the Committee will be around the villages selling balloons. Price 1/-.

A valuable prize for the winner.

SIDE SHOWS, ATTRACTIONS, Etc.

ROSE BERRY MARIONETTES.

These will perform through the afternoon and evening.

MOBILE POLICE STATION

By kind permission of the Chief Constable of Leicestershire Police.

FORTUNE TELLER.

FREAK SHOWS.

TISHA (the unrideable Horse).

ROLL THE PENNY,

Etc., etc., etc., etc.

During the whole of the afternoon and evening.

TEAS LICENSED BAR ICE CREAM REFRESHMENTS.

SPECIAL AWARDS.

The proprietors of the "Shepshed Echo" offer a valuable Challenge Cup for the winner of the Tug of War Contest.

This competition is open for any Shepshed firm or organisation.

The Challenge Cup name "The Shepshed Echo Challenge Cup for Local Charity," to be competed for annually, will be held for one year.

Sports and competitions from a Shepshed Parade and Gala souvenir programme.

eleven

Shepshed Station

William (Bill) Day, a goods checker, in the station's goods shed in July 1940. Bill died while in service in 1950, aged fifty-six. Shepshed Station was built in 1882 as part of the Charnwood Forest Railway development and was used to transport goods and passengers to and from Derby Road Station in Loughborough. It was not a financial success and the last passenger service was in 1931, but the occasional excursion train ran until the outbreak of war. Freight traffic stopped in 1964.

George Fox, on the left of the picture next to a British Railways lorry, was the last drayman serving Shepshed. Next to him is the stationmaster, J.W. Handy.

Stationmaster John William Handy. During his last few years before retirement in 1962 he had to perform almost all the tasks necessary for the running of the station. He is pictured here with a brake stick under his arm (used for pinning down wagon brakes), and making a note of empty wagon numbers. The wagons would be 'stabled' on the line between Shepshed and Loughborough Central, following the closure of Derby Road goods depot.

Unusual activity at the station, which had been closed for passengers since 1939. To celebrate its twenty-first anniversary in June 1961, the Leicester Railway Society chartered a train to take its members over seventy-eight miles of virtually disused track in Leicestershire, including the stretch between Coalville and Shepshed.

Stationmaster John Handy at his desk inside the goods office in 1961. Nothing much seems to have changed for many years, including the gas lighting. It looks cold, damp and almost Dickensian. On the desk is a heavy Bakelite telephone, a pot of Gloy liquid gum and a pencil sharpener screwed to the top. The brake stick is against the wall at left.

Shepshed Station from the Station Drive side. The archway leads to the waiting room and booking office and the window on the far right was the stationmaster's office. The window immediately left of the arch was the ladies' waiting room. The house had a lounge, dining room and three bedrooms. The single-storey extension to the left housed the kitchen and pantry (with the small square window). An outside WC and wash-house are out of the picture to the left. There was no bathroom, and during its early years water had to be carried from a tap at the bottom of the garden, some 20m away. The goods shed stands beyond the poplar tree.

This snow-covered scene shows the station from the opposite platform.

Mr Handy leads in a goods train entering Shepshed Station from Coalville, February 1962.

Stationmaster Bill Handy, on the day of his retirement on 7 July 1962, says goodbye to the guard C. Davenport, fireman Peter Beale, and driver William Aris, all from Coalville motive power depot. Bill Handy began service with the Midland Railway as a junior porter at Horton-in-Ribblesdale on 18 August 1916, where his father was stationmaster. His wages were 6s a week, with 2s 1d extra as war bonus. He became stationmaster at Melbourne in 1936 and moved to a similar post at Shepshed a year later. The locomotive pictured was an LMS 4F 0-6-0 freight engine, shedded at Coalville.

From left to right: driver William Aris, fireman Peter Beale, J.W. Handy, guard C. Davenport.

Driver William Aris takes the goods train out of Shepshed after saying goodbye to Bill Handy on the day of his retirement.

A railway station may not be everyone's idea of an ideal home, but pictured on the right of this photograph are the Matthews family who moved into the station house in 1959. The last stationmaster, J.W. Handy, had moved out in 1955, and Charles Matthews, a forty-six-year-old railway clerk at Midland Station in Loughborough, his wife Joyce and daughter Susan rented it for £1 2s per week. They were hoping to save enough to buy the property. It was demolished in 1974. From left to right: fireman Barry Gent, driver Charlie Cope, Bill Handy, guard C. Davenport, platelayer Mr Haken, Joyce Matthews, Charles Matthews, Susan Matthews.

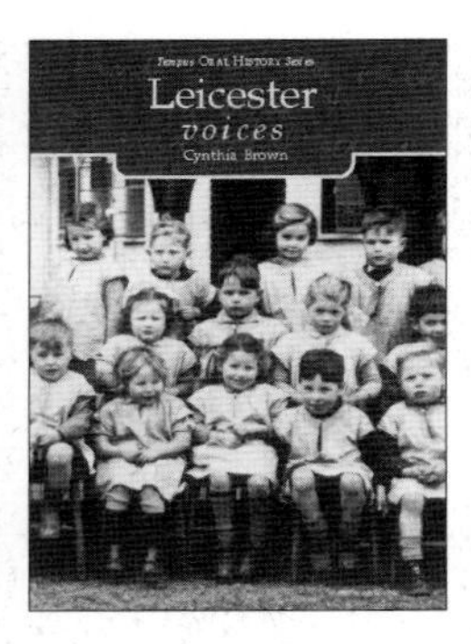

Other local titles published by Tempus

Leicester Voices

CYNTHIA BROWN

These personal memories offer a record of what life used to be like in Leicester. Selected from recordings at the East Midland Oral History Archive, each story illustrates a different aspect of life in the city as it once was. From memories of childhood and schooldays, work and family, war and peace, each extract offers an oral testimony into the lives of people who have lived in and known Leicester over the decades.

0 7524 2657 6

Around Lutterworth The Second Selection

GEOFF SMITH

This selection of over 200 old images revisits the town of Lutterworth and the surrounding villages using material from over two centuries. The book takes the reader on a tour of the area, including the bells of St Michael's in Crosby, the old windmill at Gilmorton and the Crooked Billet public house in Dunton Bassett. Aspects of everyday life are shown, with trade and industry, schools and shops, celebrations and wartime all remembered.

0 7524 2480 7

Leicestershire County Cricket Club 100 Greats

DENNIS LAMBERT

Leicestershire CCC has a mercurial history from its formation in 1879, through the second-class period, promotion to first-class status in 1894 and throughout the twentieth century. Until the mid-1970s, much of the club's time was spent in the lower reaches of the Championship. Despite the initial lack of success, there has always been talent in evidence and this book is dedicated to 100 of these remarkable players, both amateur and professional.

0 7524 2175 1

Folklore of Leicestershire and Rutland

ROY PALMER

This comprehensive volume draws upon a wide range of printed, manuscript and oral material. The topics covered include local legend and lore, ghosts and witchcraft, folk medicine, work and play, sports and fairs, crime and punishment, music, drama and calender customs. Among the many illustrations are documents and prints, archive and recent photographs and over twenty music examples.

0 7524 2468 8

If you are interested in purchasing other books published by Tempus, or in case you have difficulty finding any Tempus books in your local bookshop, you can also place orders directly through our website

www.tempus-publishing.com

or from **BOOKPOST**, Freepost, PO Box 29, Douglas, Isle of Man, IM99 1BQ
tel 01624 836000 email bookshop@enterprise.net